A
Rookie
reader®
español

Bessey, la Desordenada

Escrito por
Patricia y Fredrick McKissack
Ilustrado por Dana Regan

Children's Press®
Una División de Scholastic Inc.
Nueva York • Toronto • Londres • Auckland • Sydney
Ciudad de México • Nueva Delhi • Hong Kong
Danbury, Connecticut

Para mamá Bess que nunca es desordenada
—P. y F. M.

Asesoras de lectura

Linda Cornwell
Coordinadora de la calidad escolar y el mejoramiento profesional
(Asociación de Profesores del Estado de Indiana)

Katharine A. Kane
Asesora educativa
(Jubilada de la Oficina de Educación del condado de
San Diego y de la Universidad Estatal de San Diego)

Biblioteca del Congreso. Catalogación de la información sobre la publicación

McKissack, Pat, 1944-
    [Bessey, la Desordenada. Español]
    Bessey, la Desordenada / escrito por Patricia y Fredrick McKissack; ilustrado
por Dana Regan.
        p. cm.—(Un lector principiante de español)
    Resumen: Bessey limpia finalmente su cuarto desordenado.
    ISBN 0-516-22685-1 (lib. bdg.)   0-516-27794-4 (pbk.)
    [1. Limpieza—Ficción. 2. Orden—Ficción. 3. Comportamiento—Ficción.
4. Afroamericanos—Ficción. 5. Materiales en idioma español.] I. Título. II. Serie.
PZ73.M3722 2002
    [E]—dc21   2002067348

CHILDREN'S PRESS, AND A ROOKIE READER® y los logotipos relacionados
son marca y/o marca registrada de Grolier Publishing Co., Inc. SCHOLASTIC
y los logotipos relacionados son marca y/o marca registrada de Scholastic Inc.
1 2 3 4 5 6 7 8 9 10 R 11 10 09 08 07 06 05 04 03 02

Mira tu cuarto, Bessey, *la Desordenada*.

Mira, colores en la pared,

libros en la silla,

juguetes en el cajón del tocador

y juegos por doquier.

Bessey, *la Desordenada*,
tu cuarto es un desastre.
Mira, zapatos sobre la cama,
el abrigo en el piso,

medias sobre la mesa,
y tu sombrero en la puerta.

Bessey, mira tu cuarto desordenado.
Mira, una taza en el clóset,

galletas en la almohada,

un chicle en el cielo raso
y mermelada en la ventana.

Bessey, *la Desordenada,*
tu cuarto es un desastre.

16

17

Toma agua y jabón.
Toma el trapeador y la escoba.

A trabajar, Bessey, *la Desordenada*, tienes que limpiar tu cuarto.

De modo que Bessey fregó
y refregó las paredes,

el cielo raso

y el piso.

Tendió la cama,

recogió sus cosas

y cerró la puerta del clóset.

¡Bravo! Buena ésa, señorita Bessey.
También mírate tú.

Tu cuarto está limpio y lindo…

¡como tú!

31

Lista de palabras (75 palabras)

a	desastre	limpio	sobre
abrigo	desordenada	lindo	sombrero
agua	desordenado	medias	sus
almohada	doquier	mermelada	también
Bessey	el	mesa	taza
bravo	en	mira	tendió
buena	es	mírate	tienes
cajón	ésa	modo	tocador
cama	escoba	pared	toma
cerró	está	paredes	trabajar
chicle	fregó	piso	trapeador
cielo	galletas	por	tu
clóset	jabón	puerta	tú
colores	juegos	que	un
como	juguetes	raso	una
cosas	la	recogió	ventana
cuarto	las	refregó	y
de	libros	señorita	zapatos
del	limpiar	silla	

Acerca de los autores

Patricia y Fredrick McKissack son escritores y correctores que trabajan por cuenta propia, residentes del condado de St. Louis, Missouri. Sus premios como autores incluyen el Premio Coretta Scott King, el Premio Jane Addams Peace, el Newbery Honor y la Regina Medal de 1998 de la Catholic Library Association. Los McKissacks han escrito además *Messy Bessey and the Birthday Overnight, Messy Bessey's Closet, Messy Bessey's Garden, Messy Bessey's Holidays* y *Messy Bessey's School Desk* en la serie Rookie Reader.

Acerca de la ilustradora

Dana Regan nació y creció en el norte de Wisconsin. Se trasladó al sur a la Universidad de Washington de St. Louis y eventualmente a la ciudad de Kansas, Missouri, donde ahora vive con su esposo Dan y sus hijos Joe y Tommy.

The music stopped. The audience was on its feet, cheering!
Téo's heart felt bigger than his whole body!
He beamed out at his mom and dad, his biggest fans.

When the curtain opened, Téo's arms and legs knew just what to do. He fluttered around the stage, his costume twinkling under the warm lights. His arabesque was poised and balanced.

They walked onto the dark stage
together, hands clasped.

Ms. Lila gathered her dancers. "You look perfect, Téo," she said.

He imagined the way his hips shook like maracas when they danced the cumbia.

He remembered the *Swan lake* dancers gliding from one end of the stage to the other.

Most of all, Téo thought about how much he loved to dance.

Téo pictured himself at home,
dancing with Amma and Papí.

In his head, he heard the dhol
drum as they danced bhangra.

Amma knelt down. "These are the ways we must be brave sometimes."
Papí put his arms around Téo. "Tú eres valiente."

When Téo arrived at the recital the next day, he slowly approached his class backstage, then paused. His stomach did fouettés!

"You're ready for the stage!" Papí beamed. He took Téo's hands
and they two-stepped the cumbia forward and back. Afterward,
the boom of the bhangra dhol echoed throughout the apartment
as they all bounced and pumped their hands in the air. They held
hands and danced until dinnertime.

Amma peeked in. "Dinner's almost ready."

Just then, Téo heard his family's favorite
playlist. The shaking of maracas got
louder as he went downstairs.

Next, Téo tried on the leotard. It was soft and stretchy. The tutu fluffed out around him like a cloud as he rehearsed the recital routine. This must be how the *Swan Lake* dancers felt!

Téo loved who he saw in the mirror.

But what if the audience didn't love him back?

That night, Téo pulled on the black pants. They were so . . . plain.
The silver shirt was shiny, but it didn't *sparkle*.

Téo felt stiff, as if he couldn't get his leg
high enough for a proper arabesque!

Téo knew which costume he wanted to wear. The tutu reminded him of the peonies outside the conservatory where they saw *Swan lake*, with their layers and layers of petals.

As he grabbed his leotard, Téo felt everyone's eyes on him. This wasn't the kind of audience he wanted.

Slowly, he picked up the shirt and pants, and placed both costumes in his bag.

One day, Ms. Lila had an announcement. "Our costumes for the recital have arrived!"

The class waited excitedly for her to open the box. Small packages of sparkly lavender skirted leotards and silver shirts with black pants emerged.

"Please choose the costume you'd like to perform in," Ms. Lila said.

But arabesque was so hard.

He kept losing his balance!

At home, Téo practiced.

His arms and legs were ocean waves, flowing.

The music was the current, guiding him.
Soon, he could stand on his tiptoes in relevé.

He couldn't wait to perform onstage, under the lights in a fancy costume, before a real audience!

Each week in class, Téo learned new movements.
He loved how his ballet slippers hugged his feet
like vines coiled around a tree, and the way his
tutu swayed like the autumn breeze.

Téo's feet were light on the ground, like just fallen leaves.
He held his arms out softly as the music swirled around him.

He knew these were small but important steps,
and he wanted to get them just right.

Ms. Lila demonstrated first through fifth position.

He raised his hand.
"When do we split in the air?"

"It takes a lot of practice to perform a grand jeté," Ms. Lila answered.
"First we have to learn the basic positions."

Tinkling piano notes filled the studio as the class stretched their arms up and side to side.

They touched their toes and made butterfly wings with their legs.

Téo never knew he was so flexible!

Finn pointed to Téo's tutu. "Why are you wearing that?"
"Because it's pretty," Téo replied.
Ms. Lila smiled. "I wish I had a tutu like that!"

Ms. Lila patted the spot on the floor next to her. Téo sat down.

Téo nodded, picturing the arch of the dancers' feet in relevé, their split-straight legs as they leaped through the air, and their perfect pirouettes.

They seemed so free, floating across the stage, their costumes gleaming under the bright lights.

Amma kissed him on the forehead.
"Just enjoy dancing, like we do at home."

"Remember how excited you were when we saw *Swan lake?*" Papi asked.

As Téo peeked inside the studio,
his stomach felt topsy-turvy.